For Robert,
with a hug!

Susan
Kutrian

Messages from Amma

IN THE LANGUAGE OF THE HEART

Messages from Amma

IN THE LANGUAGE OF THE HEART

Edited by Janine Canan

CELESTIAL ARTS
Berkeley | Toronto

Celestial Arts
P.O. Box 7123
Berkeley, California 94707
www.tenspeed.com

Cover and Interior Design by Lisa Buckley

Distributed in Australia by Simon and Schuster Australia, in Canada by Ten Speed
Press Canada, in New Zealand by Southern Publishers Group, in South Africa by
Real Books, and in the United Kingdom and Europe by Airlift Book Company.

LIBRARY OF CONGRESS CATALOGING-IN-PUBLICATION DATA
Amritanandamayi, Mata, 1953-
  [Selections. English. 2004]
  Messages from Amma : in the language of the heart / edited by Janine Canan.
    p. cm.
  In English; translated from Malayalam.
  ISBN 1-58761-214-3
  1. Spiritual life--Hinduism. I. Canan, Janine. II. Title.
  BL1237.32.A3 2004
  294.5'44--dc22
                                        2003027442

First printing, 2004
Printed in Singapore

1 2 3 4 5 6 7 8 9 10 — 07 06 05 04

The words of H. H. Mata Amritanandamayi appear with the permission of the Mata Amritanandamayi Center (P.O. Box 613, San Ramon, California, 94583, tel. [510] 537-9417, www.amma.org) and the Mata Amritanandamayi Mission Trust (Amritapuri P.O., Kollam, Kerala, India, 690525, tel. [0476] 2896278, www.amritapuri.org), which are the publishers and sole copyright holders of the publications from which this collection quotes: *Amritanandam: First Twenty Issues* (M.A.M.T., 1988); *Amritavani:The eVoice of Amma* (M.A.M.T., 1/1/2000); *Awaken, Children! Dialogues with Ammachi*, Swami Amritaswarupananda (volume I, M.A.M.T, 1989; volumes 2-9, M. A. Center, 1991-1998); *The Awakening of Universal Motherhood*, Sri Mata Amritanandamayi (M.A.M.T., 2003); *For My Children: Selected Teachings of Mata Amritanandamayi* (M. A. Center, 1994); *Immortal Light: Advice to Householders*, Mata Amritanandamayi (M. A. Center, 1994); *Man and Nature*, Sri Mata Amritanandamayi (M.A.M.T., 1994); *Mata Amritanandamayi: A Biography*, Swami Amritaswarupananda (M.A.M.T., 1986); *May Your Hearts Blossom*, Sri Mata Amritanandamayi (M.A.M.T., 1993); *The Mother of Sweet Bliss*, Swami Amritaswarupananda (M.A.M.T, 1999); and *River of Love: A Documentary Drama on the Life of Ammachi*, Michael Tobias (videotape, M. A. Center, 1999).

The editor thanks Swami Paramatmananda and Swamini Krishnamrita for their kind encouragement; Prana Carpenter and Linda Johnsen for their good editorial suggestions; Anna Dreier, David English, Beverley Noia, and other photographers of Mata Amritanandamayi Math for their beautiful photographs of Amma; Attorney Steven Fleisher for his generous legal assistance; publisher Jo Ann Deck for her gracious support; and above all, Swami Amritaswarupananda, transcriber of Amma's words over many years, without whose books this collection could not exist.

Offered at the feet

of the

Divine Mother

for all her

children

Contents

Introduction

The divinely beautiful, dark Indian holy woman lovingly known by millions around the world as *Amma, the Hugging Saint, Mother of Compassion,* and *Mata Amritanandamayi, Mother of Immortal Bliss,* is one of the most extraordinary forces healing our planet today.

Born in 1953 in a poor fishing village on the tropical coast of Kerala, south India, Amma's first sound is said to have been not a cry but a laugh. She was an intensely spiritual child who spontaneously meditated and composed songs to God. Though remarkably gifted, she had to leave school at age nine when her mother became ill, and she took over the care of the family. Joyful and energetic, Sudhamani, as she was called, worked from dawn till midnight to feed and clothe her brothers and sisters and care for the animals. At night she poured out her heart in prayer and song and dance. Unable to bear seeing old people and children go hungry, she gave away family food and possessions— for which she was harshly reprimanded and beaten. But her acts of compassion continued, until finally her family threw her out of the house.

Children, read Mother's words not with your intellect but with your heart.

— AMMA

Under the coconut palms, Sudhamani lived in ecstasy, conversing with Mother Sea, hugging the trees, kissing the flowers, and rarely sleeping, eating only the milk brought by a cow, the rice delivered by a dog, and the fish dropped into her lap by an eagle. At age twenty-two, she experienced a brilliantly luminous, spinning red globe approaching her; out of it emerged the glorious form of the Divine Mother, crowned and smiling with love. The young woman's whole being rushed toward Her vibrating with the mantra *Amma, Amma, Amma (Mother, Mother, Mother)*. From this time on, Amma saw everything as divine. Eventually, the Goddess reappeared and, dazzling like a thousand suns, merged into her totally, revealing the purpose of her life: to worship God in the hearts of all beings, and to relieve the suffering of humanity.

Today Amma devotes every moment to loving and serving others. Several times a week, in cities around the world, she receives people for *darshan*, wearing a simple white sari, or on special occasions, dressed as the Divine Mother in a gorgeous colorful sari and crown. All day and all night, Amma receives people by the thousands—sometimes tens of thousands—hugging and blessing each one individually, answering their questions and wiping away their tears. Regardless of a person's race, health, wealth, education, religion or lack of it—each is accepted with the same

Come quickly,

darling children,

whose essence is divinity.

Leave behind sorrow

becoming adorable,

and merge in the Light.

Though you stumble, my children,

Mother walks beside you,

revealing the Way.

Remember in your hearts

that the Supreme Being is Love,

and meditating on its living form

you will become that Love.

fierce motherly tenderness. So far, she has embraced over thirty million people.

Out of her compassion Amma has created a vast network of charitable activities for the poor and suffering. In India she has established many innovative temples with female as well as male priests, and dozens of schools to further the integral development of creativity, academics, and character. The Holy Mother has created colleges of medicine, pharmacology, engineering, management, and computer science, as well as an outstanding vocational training center. Hospitals and clinics have been built, along with cancer and AIDS hospices, orphanages, and residences for the elderly. Amma and her foundation have established legal support for the poor, housing projects for the homeless, earthquake reconstruction for devastated villages, pensions for destitute women, rehabilitation for prostitutes, and large-scale food and clothing programs. She has inspired the creation of the Mata Amritanandamayi University, the Amrita Arts and Cultural Center, the internationally renowned Amrita Institute of Medical Sciences and Research, giving state-of-the art treatment to the very poor, as well as the Amrita Ayurvedic Research Center, specializing in traditional Indian medicine. She has inaugurated a spiritually oriented television station and numerous spiritual centers around the world that teach the principles and practice of *Universal Love*, or *Universal Motherhood*.

In this Age of Doubt, the miraculous life of Amma is a heartrendingly inspirational example of real love, beauty, sacrifice, and consciousness. "The radiant smile and total sincerity in Amma's interaction with every single person, continuously for hours," wrote one of many stunned reporters, "is astounding; the experiences of this day will remain forever etched in my memory." So moved was the president of India by Amma's work that he donated most of his annual salary. Several North American cities have honored her with special commendations. She has been invited to address the Parliament of World Religions, and interfaith celebrations in honor of the United Nations' fiftieth Anniversary. At the United Nations she addressed the Millennium World Peace Summit of World Religious Leaders, and the Global Peace Initiative of Women Religious and Spiritual Leaders, where she received the Gandhi-King Award for Non-Violence.

When Amma speaks—whether in public talks, interviews with the press, dialogues with students, personal letters, or hymns to God—it is generally in Malayalam, the beautiful mother tongue of the traditionally matriarchal Land of Kerala. Her words are transcribed and translated into English (as well as many other languages) by a variety of devoted followers, most frequently Swami Amritaswarupananda, the editor of a nine-volume series entitled *Awaken, Children! Dialogues with Sri Mata Amritanandamayi.* From his books and others, from the M. A. Center magazine, *Immortal Bliss,* as well as the biographical video, *River of Love,* are derived the quotations in this book. Passages have been selected to represent Amma's core teachings, retranslated from the original translations, organized for accessibility, and arranged for daily contemplation.

Like her love, Amma's words flow directly from the heart. Her speech is direct; and just as she wastes not a moment when she acts, she wastes not a word when she speaks. Her words are profound, often piercing, and sometimes deceptively simple. A short passage may contain truth sufficient for a lifetime. In this confused and turbulent world of ours, agitated by fear and animosity, marked by self-centeredness and violence, and starved for the all-embracing wisdom of the Mother, Amma's words come as a healing balm. Speaking directly to each of us as our own mother, as our teacher, and as the voice of our own higher Self, her words have the power to awaken, nurture, and guide us toward that truth which already lives within us all. "Love is the supreme Reality," she writes, "this is the message Mother sends you in the language of the heart."

Offered here with humility are the inspired teachings of a modern-day saint who will undoubtedly come to be known as one of the truly great spiritual leaders of all time, a woman whose life is the very incarnation of compassion. As Amma mothers the world, may we all learn to follow her extraordinary example of Love and Service.

—*Janine Canan, M.D.*

Love, the Cure

Pure Love

As the body needs food to survive

and grow, the soul needs love.

Love instills a strength and vitality

that even mother's milk cannot provide.

All of us live and long for real love.

We are born and die searching for such love.

Children, love each other and unite in pure love.

The Universal Remedy

All of us are burdened

by the sorrow and pain of past experiences.

All of us have numerous festering wounds.

The cure for these wounds

is love and compassion for others.

Love is the universal remedy.

Love Sustains

Love sustains
everything.
Love is the foundation
of the universe.

Never-Ending Stream

Things, whether money
or other objects, are gone forever
when you give them away.
But not love! The more you give,
the more your heart is filled.
Love is a never-ending stream.

Now our hearts are closed buds
that harbor anger, jealousy, and selfishness.
But when Love flows
and washes away the impurities,
our hearts will flower and bless the world.

Your Heart Is a Temple

Your heart is the temple
where God should be enshrined.
Your good thoughts are the flowers,
your good words the hymns,
your good deeds the rituals.
And Love is the offering.

The True Self

Pure Love is simply
emptying the mind of all fears,
tearing off all masks
and revealing the Self as It truly is.

✳

Love is the face
of God.

Feeling Life

Love is seeing and feeling life everywhere.
When your heart is full of love,
you sense life pulsating through all creation.

✤

You do not grow tired
when there is love.

✤

Love is the natural attitude of the soul;
it expresses the heart's longing for Divinity.

✤

You can only feel love
by expressing it.

Selfless Love

Human love arises out of selfishness.

When our desires are thwarted, it is withdrawn.

Selfless love comes only from God,

who is the embodiment of Love.

Know this and realize God.

The Source of Love

Children, go directly
to the source of Love
and drink to your heart's content
from that Ocean.

Divine Mother

Come, Mother

Come, Mother,

brilliant as millions of suns,

who dwells within,

my only hope for union.

Ambrosial light, ocean of bliss,

let my mind merge in You forever.

Absolute pure Being, to You I bow down

again and again.

Divine Mother

Every pore of my body
opened wide with longing.
Every atom vibrated the holy mantra.
My whole being rushed forth like a river
toward the Divine Mother. . .
smiling and radiant She merged into me.
All of creation I saw as one—
a tiny bubble in the vastness of Self.
And no longer did I imagine happiness
outside my own Self.

O Goddess

You are creation, You are creator,

You are energy, You are truth.

You are maker of the cosmos,

You are beginning and end.

You are energy, You are truth.

You are the soul's essence,

You are the five elements.

You are creation, You are creator,

You are energy, You are truth.

O Goddess! O Goddess! O Goddess!

All over the world Mother hears
her children's hearts calling.
She longs to soothe their painful yearnings
and lead them to eternal Light.
Mother does not distinguish among nations,
for She is everywhere—
all people are her darling children.
There are many petals on a flower but the flower
    is one—
the world is a flower and every nation a petal.
To Mother all are one.

Children,

Mother is always with you.

Whenever you think of Her,

She sees your faces.

At night She visits her children

all over the world.

Her children are her swans;

She watches and gathers the strays.

You are all baby birds

tucked under Mother's wing.

The Servant of Everyone

Do you ask why the sun shines, or the river flows?
It is Mother's nature to love—her embrace
expresses that love.

✲

An unbroken stream of love flows from Mother
to every being in the universe.

✲

Mother does not give expecting
anything in return.

✲

What nourishes Mother
is the happiness of her children.

✲

Mother is the servant of everyone.
I have no home of my own—
I live in your hearts.

When a Mother

When you are a mother,
carrying a child in your arms
or on your shoulder
is not a burden.
When your mind expands
as wide as the universe
and you experience *universal motherhood,*
even the entire world is not a burden.

Nurturing Energy

Man egotistically claims
he can push a button
and burn the world to ash
when he doesn't understand
the power that moves his own finger.

☆

We must return to the world
the nurturing energy
of the feminine.

Anyone—man or woman—
who has the courage to overcome
the limits of the mind,
can attain the state of *universal motherhood.*
The love of awakened motherhood
is a loving compassion
not only for one's own children
but for all people,
animals, plants, rocks, and rivers.
It is a love extended
to all nature's beings.
For one who has awakened to true motherhood,
every creature is his or her child.
Such love, such *motherhood,* is divine Love,
which is God.

The Inner Mother

The inner Mother,
whose true nature is silence and infinitude,
manifests through this body
so that her children may glimpse
the Mother who is within.
Whatever is expressed by this form
is *for you*, for your growth.
When through spiritual practice
you open your heart, grace will flow
and you will find Her in your own heart,
where She has always been.

Seeing the Divine Mother
in you, Amma bows down
to her own true Self.

Nature Without Error

Of Nature

Human beings
are not different from Nature,
we are part of Nature.
Our very existence on earth
depends upon Nature.
In truth, it is not we who protect Nature
but Nature who protects us.

Our Responsibility

Without Nature
no creature,
no human being,
nothing
would exist.
Thus it is
our responsibility
to lovingly care
for every living being.

The Forests

In modern times
we have chopped down
all the forests on earth
and have planted jungles
in our minds.

Nature Reacting

In the past, harmony was preserved
through religious rites
and right actions.
Now these are forgotten
and Nature is reacting.
Because there are fewer trees
there is less rain, and it falls
at the wrong time.
There is either too much
or too little sunshine.
All of this has been caused
by the selfish actions
of human beings.

Love is the foundation of the world.

Where there is love, there is peace.

Where there is selfishness,

there is misery and suffering.

Learn from Mother Nature

who gives of Herself even when exploited.

Do good and see everyone as Mother's child.

Nature's Example

How easily Nature overcomes every obstacle.

The tiny ant walks over the stone.

The roots of the tree embrace the rocks in the soil.

The river flows around every log and boulder in
    its way.

Like Nature, we should adapt to life's circumstances,

overcoming them with patience and enthusiasm.

Kill and Destroy?

God is in everything,

not only in human beings.

In the mountains, the rivers,

the trees, the birds, the animals,

the clouds, the sun, the moon, and the stars.

Everything in Nature has a purpose;

there are no errors.

Everything in God's creation is precious.

How can anyone who understands this

want to kill and destroy?

Nature Is God

Nature is
God made visible.
Nature is God
known through our senses.
When we love and serve Nature,
we are worshiping the Supreme Being.

Coolness of the breeze,
rays of the moon,
vastness of space—
everything in this world
is permeated with Divine Consciousness.

To know and experience this Truth
is the goal of our human birth.

Spiritual Education

Spiritual Education

The most important education of all
is spiritual education—
the mastery of the mind.

Spiritual Life

If you plan on taking up spiritual life
after fulfilling all your desires,
you're like the man who stands on the shore
waiting for all the waves to subside before wading in.

The Mind

The mind constantly makes waves.
And the waves cloud everything.
Each thought, desire, emotion
is like a pebble thrown into a lake.
When nothing happens in the present,
memories of the past arise—sweet pleasures,
bitter moments—joy, regret, revenge.
And when the past subsides, the future emerges
with its beautiful promises and dreams.
So the mind is continuously engaged.
But what is seen is only the surface—
when it moves, we imagine the Ground moves too.
That, however, is immovable.

The Source of the Mind

Happiness depends
not upon material comfort
but upon the mind.
Seek the source of the mind
and build your life on That.

Immersed in illusion,

we confuse what is with what is not,

and what is not with what truly is.

We view the world

through the eyes of ignorance.

We need to learn to distinguish

between the fleeting and the everlasting.

*

With eyes of ignorance

we can only see a short distance

and think there is nothing beyond.

Physical eyes can't see behind trees and walls,

or even what's in front of them in the dark.

Our senses are very limited.

As we become more conscious,

we see so much more.

We Need Spirituality

Stuck in the intellect,
we fail to get to the heart.
Since the intellect is very calculating,
we need spirituality to find our way.
Mother is not saying we should
completely eliminate the intellect,
but that we need a discriminating intellect
that distinguishes between truth and untruth.
Awareness is the most important act of all.

Self-Awareness

As heat is the nature of fire
and coolness the nature of water,
Self-awareness is the nature—
the responsibility—
of every human being
regardless of class, creed, or religion.

Opening

When a flower is only a bud,
its colorful petals cannot be seen
nor its fragrance inhaled.
But when it opens, all the petals show
and it spreads a lovely perfume.

We have the same capacity
within us—*infinite capacity*—
but are still in a closed state.
We need to open like the flower,
and spiritual understanding makes this possible.

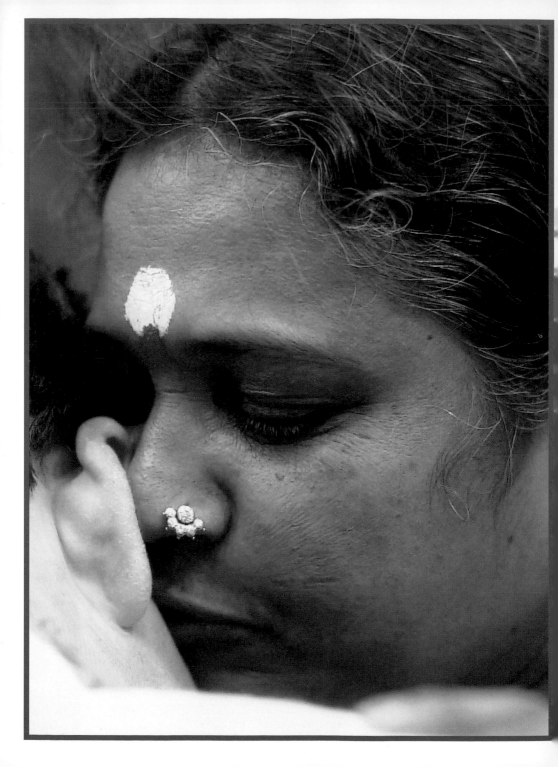

Opening the Heart

Our Biggest Problem

We tend to think only of our own problems
and not to think compassionately
of others' problems.
That is our biggest problem!

True Love

There is love, and then there is Love.

You love your family, but not your neighbor.

You love your parents, but not others' parents.

You love your religion, but not all religions—
  some you even dislike.

You love your country, but not all countries.

This is not true but rather limited love.

Transformation of limited love into Divine Love

is the goal of spirituality.

The True Meaning

Spiritual practice doesn't just mean
sitting in lotus position with your eyes closed,
but also serving the suffering,
offering a consoling smile and loving words.

Our Duty

If you enter a temple,
circle the sanctum,
place an offering in the box,
and kick the beggar at the door—
where is your devotion?

Compassion for the poor is our duty to God.

Selfless Service

Mother wants the world to know,
through her children's example,
that a life inspired by love
and service to humanity is possible.
The beauty and charm of selfless service
must never be extinguished from the Earth.

The First Step

The first step in spiritual life
is to have compassion.
A person who is kind and loving
never needs to go searching for God.
God rushes toward any heart that beats
with compassion—it is God's favorite place.

This Is Mine

When we work for someone else,
we feel unenthusiastic, avoid work, and tire easily.
When we work for ourselves, we have a
    different attitude:
we are eager and energetic,
and give up food and sleep.

If we can develop the attitude *this is mine*
toward everything,
all our problems will vanish.

Third Eye

Your third eye will never open
if, in the name of spirituality,
you close your eyes to the world.
Spiritual realization is the ability
to see yourself in all beings,
to look through the third eye
while keeping your other two eyes wide open.
The fulfillment of spirituality
is the ability to love and serve others.

There Goes God

Children, don't waste a single second.
Serve others, above all the poor,
expecting nothing in return.

✳

Just as the person who offers God flowers
is the first to enjoy their fragrance,
the person who offers compassion
is the first to receive its blessing.

✳

Wherever a heart beats
with compassion:
God is there.

Fragrant Gold

Compassion
is like *fragrant gold*—
its value is inexpressible.
Therefore, go among the sad and suffering;
love the poor and pained with all your heart.
For our greatest obligation in this world
is to serve others.

The Beautiful Flower

The beautiful fragrant flower of Compassion
blooms in the fullness of divine Love.
Compassion does not see faults and weaknesses,
or distinguish between good people and bad.
Compassion does not recognize boundaries
between nations, religions, or beliefs.
Compassion has no ego,
thus no fear, lust, or emotionality.
Compassion simply forgives and forgets—
like an open passageway. . . .
Compassion is the expression
of perfect Love.

Your True Family

Always remember
that your true family
is the family of humankind.
When your left hand is injured,
doesn't your right hand go to its aid?
For both are part of your body
and you consider them *yours.*
In the same spirit of unity
lovingly serve your sisters and brothers,
forgive their faults and be willing
to suffer for one another—
that is the essence of spirituality.

One Small Lamp

We are all links
in the chain of Life.
If one link is weak,
so is the entire chain.
Each thought and action
has the power
to brighten or darken
many lives.

Try to make others happy
and don't despair
over all the evil in the world.
Don't let others' bad actions
influence you to do wrong.
Instead of cursing the dark,
let us each light
one small lamp.

Light It

Don't be discouraged
by the impossibility of dispelling
darkness from the world
with your one little candle.
Just light it! Step forward
and let it shine with every step
you take to help others.

God Is Love

Choose a path
that benefits others
and serve with selfless love.
The supreme Reality is Love—
this is the message Mother sends you
in the language of the heart.

✶

Serving the world
with love and cooperation,
you will find your own true Self.
As you help those in need, selfishness
will fall away, and without even noticing
you will find your own fulfillment.

Let Us Open Our Hearts

We are not isolated islands,
we are connected links in a chain.
Each kind word, each smiling face,
each good action benefits our neighbor,
our community, our nation, and our world.
Let us pray and meditate together,
and we shall reach the shore of peace,
spreading the sweet holy fragrance of Love
and vibrations of unity and harmony.
Tuning our minds to the supreme Consciousness,
let us open our hearts and chant the words:
May everyone everywhere be happy.

Surrendering the Ego

The Supreme Sacrifice

To experience
supreme everlasting joy,
the supreme sacrifice is required:
the sacrifice of your ego.

The Worm of Selfishness

Selfishness is like a worm
that sucks the nectar and spoils the fruit.
If allowed to flourish, it will devour
all your good qualities.

For Others

The apple tree gives away its fruit,
keeping none: It lives for others.
The river washes all who enter,
trading cleanliness for dirt,
sacrificing itself for others.
Children, everything in this world
teaches sacrifice.
Look closely and you will see
that all of life is sacrifice.

Only a Great Blow

Surrender arises from helplessness.
Helplessness provides the opportunity
for you to release your ego.
The ego makes you feel important,
but a hopeless situation makes you realize
you are nothing and will not be free
unless you give up the sense of *I.*

This realization dawns
when you experience the burden of the ego.
Only a great blow or a serious threat
can bestow this knowledge.

Outgrowing the Ego

The difficulty is not expressing love
but letting go —*outgrowing*— the ego.
Love is human nature;
it is already present within us.
But we are held back
by our individual boundaries.
We have to outgrow our individuality
in order to become universal.
Ego stands in the way of love.
When it is removed, we can flow like a river.

Let God

When you go on a trip, you carry your bags
to the station; once on the train,
you set them down and relax.
If you have faith in the Supreme,
place all your baggage at God's feet
and let God take care of it.

The Offering

The Merciful One waits with outstretched hands
to receive your ego—
it is the only offering God asks.

But if you will not give it,
it will be taken—
for only then will you be happy.

The Bridge of Sorrow

Sorrow, my children, is the teacher
that brings you closer to God.

✧

It is God who creates the sorrows
and obstacles in a seeker's life.

✧

God employs selfish people as instruments
to make the seeker suffer.

✧

A truly spiritual person views suffering
as a blessing—a bridge to God.

✧

Without suffering
spiritual realization is impossible.

✧

Those who suffer cry more intensely to God,
creating a bridge for God to cross over.

✧

Crying out to God is certainly no misfortune—
it makes the heart blossom.

Understand this great truth:
The happiness that comes
from the pleasures of the world
is but a minute reflection of the infinite bliss
that comes from within your own Self.

The Greatness of Humility

Like a seed buried in earth to sprout into a tree,
a human being must be modest and humble
in order to grow spiritually.

✻

Nothing is gained by egotistical confrontations,
feeling important, thinking we know everything,
have nothing to learn and can defeat any argument.

✻

Only after we ourselves have become good
are we in a position
to give advice to others.

✻

Pride and selfishness will destroy us,
but if we feel love and compassion as if we are
everyone's servant, the whole universe will bow down.

✻

Rain upon the mountain streams downhill
pooling in the ravine at the bottom.
So great is humility, everything rushes toward it.

✶

In asking for surrender—*total surrender*—
to the supreme Self, spirituality
shows us the way to lasting happiness.

✶

Surrender to the Supreme
is the only guarantee of safety
and the only way to bliss.

✶

When huge trees are uprooted by a cyclone
and tall buildings collapse, the grass remains
unscathed—such is the greatness of humility.

✶

Take it to be Divine will,
and there will be
no problem.

✶

When we offer ourselves to the Divine,
our minds are purified, sorrows end,
and life becomes a festival.

✶

Humility
is the sign
of true knowledge.

Your Divine World

O divine Spirit, do You see me here?

May your starry hands shower grace upon me—

the strength to keep remembering You

and the sorrow to keep calling You,

my only refuge and comfort.

Blissful, oh beautiful is your divine world!

Lift me to your world of a million twinkling stars.

Hiding the Sun

Mother says, the little self
is like a bunch of gray clouds
hiding the Sun.

A Guiding Light

A Guide

If we trust a guide to take us
to a place unknown in the outer world,
why not trust a realized Soul to lead us
to that ultra-subtle mysterious world within?

The Shade of a Tree

There is a *guru* in everyone,
but to survive and grow
it requires protection
from a realized Teacher—

as a seedling requires
shelter from a full-grown tree
to avoid withering and dying
in the scorching sun.

The Guidance

A seeker cannot remove
subtle negative tendencies alone.
To overcome negative habits
we need the guidance, instruction,
and grace of a true master.

True Master

By *true master*, we do not mean a mere individual;
we mean divine Consciousness, the Truth.
The master permeates the whole universe:
only if this is understood can we advance spiritually.

Students should not be attached to the master's body.
We should widen our view to encompass
every sentient and insentient being as *master.*
We should serve all beings with devotion.

Bonding to *the master,* we gain this expansiveness.
A mind matured by listening to the master's words
and observing the master's actions
will rise to this plane of consciousness.

The Teacher Appears

When love catches fire, the beloved comes.
When the student wakes, the teacher appears.

✧

People who wander from teacher to teacher
are not ready for spirituality.

✧

When you find a shop that has all you need,
why roam every shop in the marketplace?

✧

Your mind isn't prepared to know the Supreme,
but a teacher can help make it ready.

✧

The attitude of reverence helps us advance,
but the bond to a teacher helps even more.

✧

Experiencing the presence of a realized master
is like being reborn.

✶

Simply by being in the presence
of a master, we open up.

✶

Surrender grows from the vast inspiration
of the teacher's physical presence.

✶

The master destroys obstacles
and reveals to the seeker the sacred path.

✶

One who has seen divinity
can show us how to see divinity too.

✶

Because the master has a universal mind,
the master knows what we need.

✻

The teacher knows which practice and path
the disciple needs: action, knowledge, or devotion.

✻

Faith in the teacher and her words
protects us like a mother.

✻

As water flows downhill, the teacher's grace
naturally flows toward the person with faith.

✻

As a mother loves her baby,
the teacher showers pure selfless love.

✵

To the teacher we may tell all our sorrows—
she does not get angry but guides us with love.

✵

Faith in our teacher gives us the mental strength
to overcome every obstacle on the path.

✵

A true master is an endlessly loving alchemist
who transforms students into pure gold.

✵

The master, like a sculptor, chips away the stone
to reveal the divine Self buried within.

Into the Cup

Into the cup of the intellect
pour devotion,
and drink!

Ever Burning

The teacher is an ever-burning lamp
by whose light we can watch the mind and senses.

The teacher enlightens not through her words
but through the example of her life.

The teacher wakes the student who wishes
to open his or her heart to the teacher.

Only when the student loves the teacher
with real devotion will the mind awaken.

The ego must be removed; this painful process
is only possible through surrender to the teacher.

The teacher breaks the ego's shell, and the disciple rises
like a banyan tree, giving shade to the world.

A Real Guru

A real guru destroys ignorance;
kindles and sustains in the student
the light of spiritual knowledge.

A real guru works with a student's habits,
creates awareness of negativities
and helps remove them.

A real guru is not interested in psychic powers,
having all the powers she needs,
is simple and humble.

A real guru is a realized soul
who embodies the eternal virtues:
love, renunciation, patience, forbearance, endurance.

A real guru has equal regard for all
and perfect mental balance,
selflessly desiring only creation's welfare.

A real guru does not criticize,
for her nature is tranquility; she uses
anger to correct and guide, not dominate.

A real guru's anger is an expression of love
that falls away like a burnt shell,
leaving her mind unmoved.

A Spiritual Master

A master teaches us to accept everything,
be thankful for good and bad, right and wrong,
friend and enemy, helper and abuser, liberator
    and oppressor.

A master helps us to forget the dark past
and the future bright with a thousand promises,
and live in the fullness of the present moment.

A master shows us how all of Nature,
every being, every thing—even our enemy—
helps us evolve and attain perfection.

A Living Example

A spiritual master embodies all the divine qualities.
In her, or him, one finds true surrender and
  acceptance.
A master is a living example.

Only through the vast compassion
of a realized master
can we experience God tangibly.
In the presence of a master we come to know
that God really exists.

Practicing
Remembrance

Spiritual Practice

Spiritual practice is *crucial.*

As the seed of the plant

only bears fruit if rightly cultivated,

the Truth of the human being

only shines brightly through spiritual practice.

The Blueprint

The person who constantly studies
without doing spiritual practices
is like the fool who attempts to live
in the blueprint of a house.

Those who believe in Mother
may meditate on Her;
those who believe in Christ
may meditate on Him;
those who have no deity
may meditate on a flame or a dot.
Those who love Nature
may meditate on the moon,
or imagine merging into a flowing river,
a beautiful bright sky or a lake.
Or imagine that you are God
and meditate on That.
Concentration is the important thing:
Meditation is constant remembrance of God.

The Great Ideals

Our gross minds cannot imagine the Supreme
without form, attributes, or story.
We need a Rama, a Krishna, a Buddha, or a Christ
to embody supreme qualities
and give us a form to worship.
But when we say that the Supreme incarnates
in Rama, Krishna, or Christ,
and we develop a relationship with Him,
it is *not* his body we worship
but the great ideals He embodies.

Meditating on a divine form will help you
develop concentration and mental purity.

The pure aspect of your beloved divinity
will grow within you without your realizing it.

Love for a formless God rarely develops
as easily as for a God you can visualize.

Following the path of knowledge without love
and devotion is like eating stones.

Formless all-powerful God readily assumes a form
for the sake of the devotee.

With complete faith and confidence
in your beloved deity, you will reach the goal.

In Every Object

See every object
as your beloved deity.
When holding a book,
handling clothes, or opening a door,
mentally bow to the beloved divinity
who stands before you.

At Night

Meditating in the daytime
is half as valuable as meditating at night,
when the atmosphere is calm and quiet
and worldly vibrations are few.
The pure air that rises from the flowers
and the absence of worldly thoughts
create an atmosphere conducive to meditation.

Our Bodies and Our Minds

Children, eat to live,
sleep to awaken.

✻

The kind of food we eat
appears in our bodies and in our minds.

✻

A real meditator is not a slave to food
but its master.

Meditation

Meditation is not just sitting
with your eyes closed.
It is a state of unbroken concentration—
like an endless stream.

*

Meditating and repeating God's name
without concentration
is like putting stamps on an envelope
without an address.

*

Thoughts are as hard to stop
as the waves of the ocean,
but they will naturally subside
as your mind expands and deepens.

*

The concentration we need to count
every grain in a handful of sand,
or to walk over a river on a rope,
is the concentration we need in every action.

✲

Work selflessly, with your whole heart,
pouring yourself into everything you do.
Let your work become your spiritual practice
and your actions will carry you to the source of Bliss.

✲

Never give up your practice
over momentary frustration or disappointment.
The results of practice are never lost.
They remain within you, ready to bear fruit at the
    right time.

Sincerely

Even a little spiritual practice
done sincerely
will produce results.

Pay Attention

To take a boat beyond the waves,
the fishermen row hard,
paying attention to nothing else.
People wave from the shore
crying out encouragement,
but the boatmen ignore them.
They have only one thought:
to get past the heaving waters!

Children, now you are
in the midst of the waves
and will only reach the goal
if you pay attention to nothing else.
Otherwise, the water will sweep you up
and toss you over.

Remember

Remember:
Mother is always with you.
Love each other,
serve others selflessly.
And never forget to do your practices.

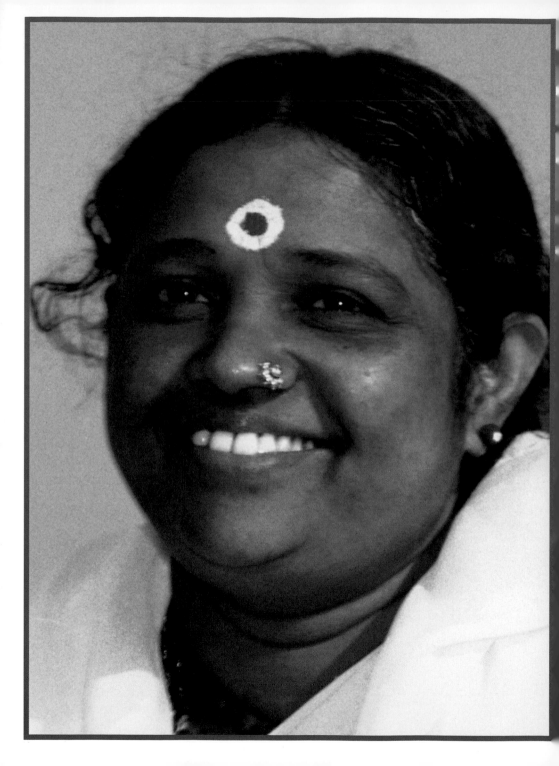

Seeing the Good

Honeybee

Be like the honeybee
who gathers only nectar
wherever it goes.
Seek the goodness
that is found in everyone.

Be Optimistic

My child, never lose faith
in God or life.
It is very important to be optimistic.
Pessimism is a form of darkness
that prevents the Divine Light
from penetrating your life.
It is an illusory curse
created by the illusory mind.
Only if you are optimistic
will you be able
to perceive that life
is replete with Divine Light.

God's Child

You are the child of God,
and God would never close
all the doors around you.
They may appear shut
but they have been left slightly ajar.
Just knock, and they will give way.

How Can God Resist

If you take each step
with good thoughts in your mind
and a smile on your face,
goodness will come
and fill your being.
Then how can God resist?
She will embrace you,
and every moment will bring you
peace and happiness.

Never Blame

If you fall into a hole,
you don't poke out your eyes
because they have failed you.
Why not tolerate others' faults as well?

When you hurt your hand
you don't reproach it,
you apply medicine and nurse it with care.
So too should we care for others
never blaming them for their faults.

The Good Qualities

We tend to look for the flaws
and errors in others,
and this disturbs our minds.
We must change this habit.
Forget their shortcomings,
look for their good qualities,
and be respectful.
Seeing only what is good in people
eliminates suffering.

Rejoice

Do not be angry.
Always rejoice in God.

✢

Words should give love and warmth,
not heat and smoke.

✢

Every day of the year should be joyful—
all of life a festival!

Rise to a Higher Level

Dwelling on another's faults
weakens the mind.
When we choose to see another's goodness,
we rise to a higher level.
In calling another human being *bad,*
we too turn bad.
Even in someone who is ninety-nine percent bad,
see the one percent that is good—
and you will become good.

Like a Tree

A seeker should be like a tree
that offers shade even to the man
who chops it down.

Only if we pray for the good of others,
even those who persecute us—are we truly
　　spiritual.

See Only God

Like the wind that blows equally
over fragrant flowers and stinking dung,
spiritual people are not only attracted to the friendly
and hostile to the unfriendly.
For them, both are of equal value.
In everyone they see only God.

Our Thoughts

The mind is nothing but thoughts.
Strong thoughts become actions; repeated actions
become habits; and habits become character.
To dissolve the mind we must change our thoughts.

✻

It's not easy to eliminate the flow of thoughts—
that is an advanced state—but by increasing
pure thoughts, impure thoughts
can be decreased and eventually eliminated.

✻

If pure water is poured into salt water,
the water gradually loses its saltiness.
In the same way, good thoughts
will gradually dissolve our bad habits.

Practice
seeing only the good
in others.

✻

With a change of attitude
you will be able to see goodness
everywhere you look.

✻

Imagine that each person is sent by God,
and you will be able to be kind
and loving to everyone.

✻

If you try to see the good
in everyone,
others will follow your example.

If we are alert,

we can learn from everything.

Everything becomes our teacher.

Just absorb the divine essence

and discard the rest.

Discrimination

A sculptor sees an image to be carved
where others find only wood and stone.

A seeker, distinguishing the eternal
from the ephemeral, chooses the Everlasting.

Awareness

The world is a slippery rock—
step carefully, or you will fall.
Proceed on life's journey with awareness.

✡

Children, all of spirituality
is contained in that one word:
Awareness.

Entering the Stream
of Grace

Effort and Grace

Effort and grace are interdependent;
without one, the other is impossible.

✱

Half by humanity, half by God, said the sages.
Effort is humanity's half, and grace is God's.

✱

Nothing is gained without effort, but the effort
is all we make—the result comes from God.

✱

No matter how hard we work,
nothing is attained without God's grace.

Grace Is Beyond

The sense of *I* and *mine*
dominates modern society.
People believe they can achieve
everything by human effort.
This idea is erroneous.
Of course we must put forth effort,
but we must also pray for grace,
for that is the deciding factor
and without it nothing is achieved.
Human effort is in our hands,
but grace is not—grace is beyond.

Ready for Grace

To receive God's grace
we must surrender totally to God.

✲

When we stop being selfish,
we are ready for God's grace.

✲

God is always with those who
make a sincere effort and have the right attitude.

✲

For every step you take toward God,
God will take a hundred steps toward you.

✲

Liberation means stepping into
the stream of Grace. . . .

Meaningful Work

No work is meaningless.

It's the amount of love—of heart—

you pour into your work that determines

how beautiful and meaningful it will be.

Through Action

We are not perfect at birth—
we progress only through action.

✻

If you hold on to a seed, it won't sprout—
you must plant it!

✻

Instead of waiting for others to improve,
try to improve yourself.

Toddlers Who Fall

Failure is
a natural part of life.

⚹

Accept failure as an experience
you need for your growth.
Be glad that some karma is complete.
See your failure as a lesson, learn from it,
and move on.

⚹

We don't worry about where the river came from
as we travel downstream—nor is there any reason
to worry about mistakes made in the past.
Instead, try to shape the future.

⚹

Every failure brings a message of success.
Like toddlers who fall when learning to walk,
we fail on our way to victory.

Good Actions

Our actions in past lives
have created what we call our *fate.*
Though fate is certainly powerful,
it can be overcome in part
by good actions in the present.

✳

As a stone thrown into the air
may be caught before hitting the ground,
the result of an action
may be altered in its course.
Thus there is no need to brood over fate.

The fruits of our actions depend upon many factors,
and all of these upon God's grace.
That is why Mother says our only hope
is to seek refuge at God's feet.

✻

Though you have done a hundred good actions,
if you make one mistake, people reject you.
But if you make a hundred mistakes
and do only one good deed, the Divine embraces you.

Tapping into Grace

We need to learn the art of tapping in
to that unknown source of grace.
For grace we must do good actions,
helping others with a kind and loving attitude.
It is important to understand
that *spirituality is life*—not just words,
something to talk about and then forget.

Faith

Faith is important

because the spirituality of love and higher values

is abstract; it can't be seen,

it's a feeling, a subjective experience.

All of life rests in faith.

For each step forward we need faith.

Faith creates a flow,

which inundates the entire universe.

The Blissful Self

In You

Amma sees a Mother, a Buddha,
a Rama, a Krishna, or a Christ
hidden in each of you.
Divine light can dawn
within you at any moment—
it simply waits for the right time.

Hear That Sound

There's a flute inside you.
Try playing it!
Once you hear that sound,
you are free from birth and death.

The Flow of the Heart

A beautiful song arises only
when the singer forgets herself and the audience.
A deeply moving painting emerges only
when the artist forgets himself and everything
    else in the world.
For your talents to be expressed in all their full-
    ness and beauty,
the sense of *otherness* must disappear entirely—
or it will block the flow of your heart.

When Your Mind Expands

There is only one all-pervading Self.
When your mind expands,
you will merge with It.
The selfish ego will disappear
and all will be one.

Reaching the Absolute

A person has reached the Absolute
when there is no feeling of hatred,
no perception of superiority or inferiority.

Everything is within us—we *are*
the absolute Self—but the words
are not enough, we must have the experience.

The jackfruit and its seed are both sacred,
but the fruit is sweet and the seed is not—
first it must sprout, grow into a tree, and bear
    fruit.

We can reach the Absolute if we try,
but why call ourselves God when we run after food
and clothing as if our bodies were immortal?

Look at the great Souls who guide the world
without hostility, mingle joyfully with everyone,
and view every being as equal.

Realization

Realizing God
is nothing but the ability—
the expansiveness of heart—
to love everything
equally.

All-Pervading Self

Those who reside in the supreme Self
see the Divine at work in everything.
They see pure Consciousness
unstained by illusion.
As a sculptor sees in a stone
the image to be carved,
great Souls see in all that exists
the all-pervading Self.

Shining Light

When you experience only God,
your whole life is an act of worship,
a form of prayer, a song of praise.
You see enlightenment, dormant,
in everyone who comes before you.
You see the inmost Self and feel deep reverence.
Nothing is insignificant; everything has meaning.
Even in a blade of grass
you see supreme Light shining.

The Soul That Realizes

The soul that transcends the body and realizes
    the Self
experiences no distinctions—everything partakes
of universal Consciousness, is interconnected,
inseparable, part of the whole.

The realized soul experiences itself everywhere—
here, there, above, below, in every direction,
in the ugly as well as the beautiful.
Wherever it goes, the Self is there!

Always aware, never unaware,
functioning spontaneously from deep within,
the soul sees no strangers,
for it *is* the all-pervading Consciousness.

Know Your Self

When you know you are the Self,
you are like a giant battery
connected to a cosmic power supply
providing constant, inexhaustible strength.

When you are connected to the Self,
the source of all power,
your energy never diminishes;
you draw from an infinite potential.

Be aware of your immense strength.
You are not a meek little lamb
but a majestic, powerful lion!
You are the cosmic energy of almighty God.

Bliss Forever

God is pure bliss!
Happiness is limited, but bliss is limitless,
beyond everything—it is
the very nature of God.

The instant you realize God,
you will be established in supreme bliss forever.

In Everyone

You don't have to go searching for God—
God shines in everyone!
There isn't more of God somewhere
in India or even in Heaven
than in You.

Think of God
as your own Self.

One Truth

Pure Experience

There is a Power
we cannot express in words,
which we call *God.*
We often say, *God is within,*
but what use are these words?
Only through intuitive experience
can we know God.

✽

God
is a subjective experience
beyond the intellect.
It is *Pure Experience.*
Like electricity,
It cannot be seen
but It can be *felt.*

The Source

The lovely melody of a flute
is found neither in the instrument
nor in the player's fingers.
You might say it comes from the composer's heart,
but if you opened his heart
you would find no melody.
Where, then, is the source?
It is beyond—in the supreme cosmic Energy
which the ego will never know.
Only if you act from your heart
will you know life's divine power.

Beauty

Isn't beauty
the very nature
of divine Consciousness?

Giver of Everything

God is the giver of everything
and does not need or want
anything from us.

*

God is a giver,
who gives like the sun.
The sun does not need light
from a candle.

In God

God hears all our prayers,
though the One who pervades all things
and knows all thoughts
does not need to hear them.
Whether we know it or not,
our thoughts already exist in God.

Man or Woman

Is God a Man or a Woman?
The answer to the question is
Neither—God *is That.*
But if you must give God a gender,
God is more female than male,
for *he* is contained in *She.*

Divine Will

Behind everything—blooming flowers,
singing birds, blowing winds,
burning fires—is Divine will.
Divine will is the cause
of the birth, growth, and death
of all beings and all creation.
It is the supreme Energy
that sustains the universe.
Without It, the world would not exist.

Satchitananda

The ocean of Consciousness
is undivided *being—awareness—bliss.*
Great souls are the waves,
and ordinary people are the bubbles.

There Is Only One

There is an infinite power independent of
and transcending every created thing.
That power is God, and there is only one.

*

Christians call God *Christ*;
Muslims call God *Allah*;
Hindus call God *Shiva, Krishna, Mother*—
but *all* are the same God.

*

There is only one God.
The supreme Self says, *However
you conceive of me, I am there.*

*

The many forms of God portrayed by the sages
were meant to accommodate different tastes and
   temperaments,
not to imply that there really are different Gods.

✣

There is no difference in the electricity
that runs through the refrigerator, fan, or lamp.
One pure Being runs through everything.

✣

There is only one
supreme Truth
shining through all religions.

If you see God as the grass,

God appears as that.

If you see God as a stone,

God appears as that.

If you see God as a buffalo,

God appears as that.

But however you conceive of God,

you need faith.

God Returns

All-knowing,
all-powerful,
all-pervading
Consciousness
assumes a form.
And when its purpose
is accomplished,
like ice melting into water
God returns
to pure formless Being.

The Divine is present in everyone,
in all beings, in everything.
Like space It is everywhere,
all pervading, all powerful, all knowing.
The Divine is the principle of life,
the inner light of consciousness,
and pure bliss—
It is our very own Self.

One

Life

and

God

are

One.